The Isobath inkwell, made by Royal Doulton, with a hemispherical float to keep the ink in the dipping well at a constant level.

WRITING ANTIQUES

George Mell

Shire Publications Ltd

CONTENTS

Printed in Great Britain by C. I. Thomas & Sons (Haverfordwest) Ltd, Press Buildings, Merlins Bridge, Haverfordwest, Dyfed.

COVER: *A rosewood writing box with a letter holder, letter balance, taper canister and other accessories.*

BELOW: *An expert quill cutter at work. The actual cutting takes only a few minutes, but the feather must be cleaned and hardened first.*

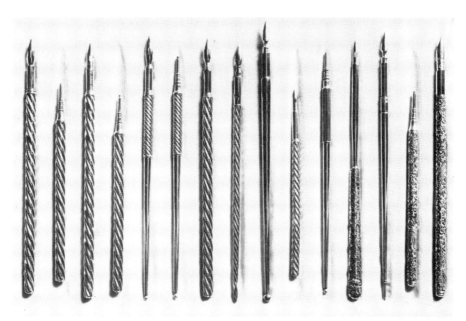

Pens and pencils with barley-sugar twist holders or barrels were quite popular in Victorian times, although they could not have been comfortable to hold.

INTRODUCTION

Writing originated as picture writing, in which a picture, at first drawn as a simple representation, through repetition became a stylised symbol associated with a specific word. At this stage it became possible to use a symbol to represent an idea or process, as the Egyptians conveyed 'running' with a bent leg and 'seeing' with a wide-open eye. The Chinese saw no need to go further and refined and developed their ideographic writing.

The Sumerians passed their cuneiform, (wedge-shaped) script – the earliest form of writing – to neighbouring races, where it developed in different ways. In one group symbols came to represent syllables and, later, individual sounds only. The use

of such alphabetic writing slowly spread to the east – to India, and to Asia Minor and Greece.

Developments in language had a relationship to the writing surfaces and tools. The Sumerians developed a symbolic script not least because they were incising wet clay with a wedge-shaped reed. The Chinese kept their writing an art form by writing with a brush. Although reed and paper were also used, the Romans did much of their writing on wax tablets with a stylus, which helps to account for the late development of lower-case letters in Latin writing, without which the cursive, flowing style of modern writing could not develop.

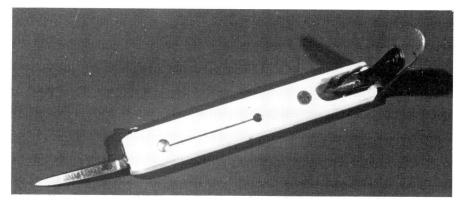

ABOVE: *A quill pen cutter. The casing is ivory and the penknife is retractable.*

BELOW: *An assortment of unusual nibs. Those at each end are for writing scripts that run from right to left. The one with five points is for ruling the lines of the musical stave. The outsize nibs and the hand-shaped example are typical of the novel shapes of the pen and ink era.*

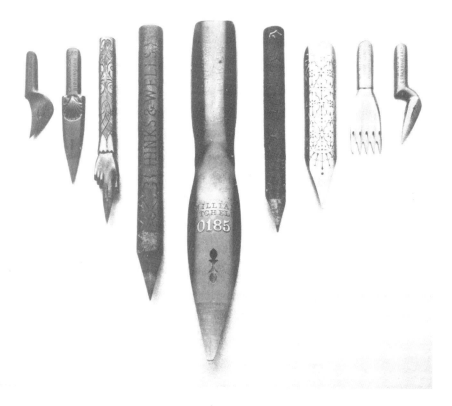

These nibs embossed with likenesses of famous people, British and foreign, were made to stimulate sales abroad. They include Garibaldi, King Charles of Wurtemburg, Schiller, Charles Dickens, Princess (later Queen) Alexandra, Elizabeth of Germany and the Swiss emblem.

PENS AND NIBS

The Egyptians used a sharpened reed to write on papyrus. Specimens found in tombs show that a new pen was probably 10 inches (250 mm) long, but it was recut as the point was blunted, until it ended as a 2 inch (50mm) stub. The Romans tried a form of metal pen which proved too inflexible for general use. The quill pen (from *penna,* Latin for a feather) was first used about the fifth century and quills cut from the wing feathers of geese, swans, peacocks, crows and turkeys were widely used until the nineteenth century.

The point was cut to the shape of a modern nib and was similarly slit upwards for flexibility in writing. The pen was very supple, especially when used on vellum (fine parchment made from calfskin), but soon lost its point and needed to be recut with a penknife made specially for the purpose. The early penknife, which usually had an ivory handle and a short but very sharp blade, developed into the folding knife we know today. Sir Walter Scott is said to have written a complete novel with a goose quill.

About 1823 some nibs were cut from horn and tortoiseshell, softened and reinforced with chips of diamond, ruby and other gemstones for greater durability. They made little impact for, in 1832, no less than 33,668,000 quill pens were in use in Britain, most imported from the continent.

The invention of the quill cutter machine early in the nineteenth century enabled a quill to be cut to a perfect point and slit in the middle for flexibility in writing. These machines were made in ebony, ivory and in some cases silver, and they incorporated a sharp, usually retractable, knife for first trimming the feather and in later models a small guillotine mechanism for trimming the point for different styles of writing. They can still be found but are quite rare.

Although quills almost disappeared when the steel nib was perfected they can still be bought. A London shop, which sells little other than pen nibs, cuts quills as required and several London banks supply them if customers ask.

The real revolution in writing began when the first steel nibs appeared, inflexible and scratchy as they were at first and susceptible to the corrosive agents in ink. The Perryian 'Regulating Spring Pen', made about 1843, was fitted with a sliding spring to regulate flexibility, while another model had a thin rubber band round the nib for the same purpose. About the same time Joseph Gillott patented his improved nib, which did not broaden with use. On his wedding morning he and his bride to be made a gross, which they sold to guests at a shilling each! The takings, about £4, helped the happy couple to a good start in married life.

Gillott began to mass-produce them and prices fell from 40p per gross to 20p and then to only 1½p per gross. The introduction of the penny post created a boom in letter writing, while in schools children were given paper and dip pens instead of slates and slate pencils. Copying alphabets from hornbooks became a thing of the past. Millions of pens and nibs were sold and Gillott made a fortune.

Despite their simple shape pen nibs were produced in endless variety. Slits were cut in the shoulders to hold more ink. Points were fine, medium or broad or were cut to suit left-handed writers. Special nibs were made for lettering, mapping, italic lettering, poster work, sketching or writing on cloth. Some nibs had three points for ruling cash columns, while musicians using five-pointed nibs could rule their own musical staves.

Non-corrodible nibs sold at 1½p for a box of nine. The Golden J (2p per dozen) could, it was claimed, write a whole letter with one dip of ink. Many nibs had fancy names. The Duke, 'specially adapted for writing paper of any texture', the Carbon Oblique Slip, the Gilt Flange, the Figaro, the Times, the International and many more each claimed a special quality. Nor were those the only variations. Nibs were embossed with likenesses of Queen Victoria, Bismarck, Napoleon and other celebrities. One was shaped like a hand, others were pierced with filigree patterns and one made in France was even shaped like the Eiffel Tower.

Salesmen carried hundreds of different nibs, in special wallets, for the stationers to select from. In the more expensive stores gold nibs cost between 25p and £1.05 and could be repaired for about half

The giant 'hand' nib, several inches long.

6

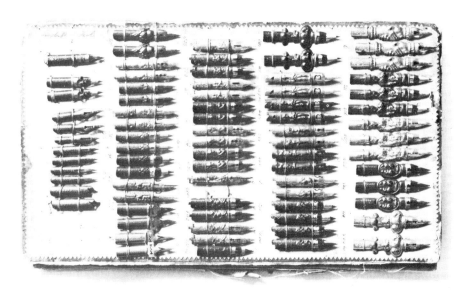

ABOVE: *A page from a traveller's wallet, which contained several other sheets filled with different nibs.*

BELOW: *A few of the decorative boxes in which pen nibs were sold. They were made in Birmingham, except for the second and third on the bottom row, which were made in Germany and Italy respectively.*

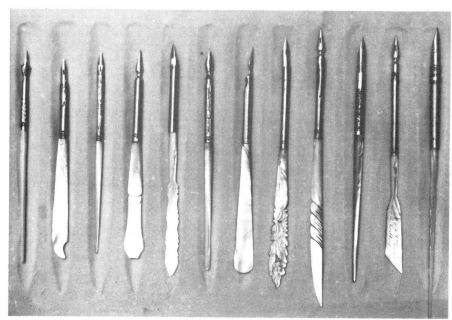

ABOVE: *A selection of pens with decorative mother of pearl holders. The second from the right is engraved with the owner's name.*

BELOW: *A pen made entirely of glass. Judging from the advertisement it had every known virtue.*

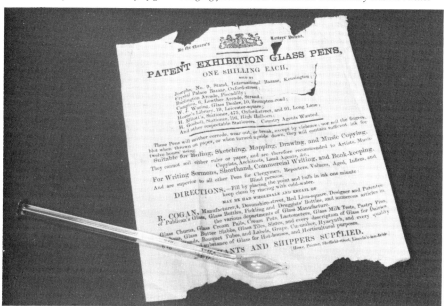

8

Fountain pens often come up for sale in specialist auctions. This selection shows pens from 1885 to the present time.

the original cost. Even the boxes in which nibs were sold were often sufficiently decorative to be worth collecting and many have survived intact.

At first steel nibs were attached to the end of quill pens but soon pen-nib holders were produced, in all shapes and sizes and every adaptable material; the scope for novelty and variation was enormous. The cheapest were made of wood, often brightly coloured and patterned. Most were cylindrical but some were waisted or triangular. The holder might incorporate 'a firm and comfortable rubber grip for the finger – no more writer's cramp' or accommodate any style or size of nib. One was made as a perpetual calendar; others were shaped for use as paper knives. Enterprising advertisers ordered pens for free distribution bearing their names and addresses and in holiday resorts pens marked 'A present from . . .' were sold as souvenirs. More expensive holders were made in engraved mother of pearl, silver, gold, porcelain, agate, tortoiseshell, glass and ivory. A popular ivory souvenir holder had a hole in the tip into which were set three or four tiny pictures of the resort.

Long before the invention of steel nibs writers had craved a pen which could hold its own supply of ink. Several gadgets were devised for use with quill pens – Samuel Pepys owned some sort of 'reservoir pen' – but none was satisfactory or widely used. In 1819 the 'Penographic Fountain Pen' appeared in which the 'ink feed to the nib is controlled by a cock which must be closed before the cap can be replaced on the pen. Accidental leakage is thus prevented.' The first self filler, invented by J. J. Parker in 1823, consisted of a hollow reservoir containing a piston which drew up the ink by suction into the tube. Other types were marketed but all suffered from the same fault, leakage.

The breakthrough was not made until 1883. Lewis Edson Waterman, a New York insurance agent, had persuaded a wealthy prospective client to sign his policy form. Waterman produced his fountain pen and disaster followed: ink poured on to the form and ruined it. While Waterman was away collecting another form a rival agent forestalled him. So Waterman decided to invent a pen that would never leak.

Within three years he discovered the

capillary attraction system, which is still the basic method of filling fountain pens. With his new pen he had no more accidents and he soon realised that the pen aroused more interest than his policies so he began to manufacture pens at home. He sold nine hundred in the first year, and, when a small advertisement in a magazine produced a flood of orders, he became a full-time fountain-pen manufacturer and made a fortune. Their function does not permit much variation in shape, but they can be found in Bakelite, vulcanite and other plastics, silver, gold and base metals and glass. Some have retractable nibs or barley sugar twist barrels. Small ones were made for women's handbags and were often decorated with gold bands or had barrels of mother of pearl. Several collections of fountain pens have been sold at Christie's, South Kensington, including a glass one made in 1849. Many pens made between 1920 and 1950 were bought by eager collectors.

Ink was sold in treacle-brown stoneware bottles like the one on the left. The Waterman bottle, containing better ink, is protected by a wooden canister with a screw top.

A few of the many types of ink bottle that were thrown away when empty and are now recovered by collectors from old rubbish dumps.

INK AND INK BOTTLES

Originally ink was made by combining lampblack with gum and a little water and forming the mixture into small sticks or cakes which were dried in the sun and later dissolved when required. This is the basis of Indian ink, which, despite its name, was invented in China. Being water based, it was easily washed off papyrus, parchment or paper, so vinegar was substituted for water and the writing became 'fixed'. Various substances were added to make different colours and for centuries scribes made their own inks, based on their favourite recipes.

In the eighteenth and nineteenth centuries chemists made ink and sold it in bottles, but it could also be bought from street vendors, whose donkeys carried ink in barrels. About 1834 Henry Stephens began manufacturing 'a carbonaceous black writing fluid which will accomplish the so long-desired and apparently hopeless task of rendering the manuscript

as durable and as indelible as the printed record. It is proof against every known chemical agent, and combines with the paper and parchment so strongly as to resist moisture and every other influence.'

Perry and Company advertised their 'Perryian Limpid Ink' which had 'a flowing property peculiar to itself and does not corrode Metallic Pens as other Inks'. This was also available in powder form, which was very popular with schools and institutions. The discovery of aniline dyes some years later enabled the corrosive constituents of ink to be removed and the need for pen and quill cleaners vanished.

Ink bottles are best found in Victorian rubbish dumps. Being neither artistic nor expensive they were thrown away when emptied and now bottle collectors dig them up. Most were made of glass or brown earthenware, occasionally in pottery, and in enough shapes and sizes to offer a wide field of interest for the impecunious collector. Pottery bottles were usually round or square, but glass ones took many different forms. They can be octagonal with perpendicular or sloping sides, have bevelled shoulders, bear the maker's name on the side, base or foot rim, or have fluted or ribbed sides. Some were made in the shape of locomotives, houses or boots. Others were described as 'teapot' bottles because the pen had to be dipped in a spout. In some instances the pen aperture was offset.

Several types had ridges on them for use as pen rests, while a few had a recess in the side to hold a free-gift pen nib. Rather unusual are the barrel-shaped ink bottles, most made to stand upright, although a few were designed to rest on their sides. Porcelain bottles often had all four sides decorated with hand-painted pictures and, for the fastidious, during the late eighteenth and nineteenth centuries, perfumed ink was sold in glass-stoppered bottles.

Bottle collectors learn to recognise the niceties of these relics, taking note of whether the pouring lip was applied after the bottle had been made or whether it was 'sheared' (roughly cut or broken off), leaving a jagged edge.

Ink for schools was usually supplied in larger quantities to be decanted into the familiar inkwells set into desks. Most of these bottles were made of earthenware but some were made of glass, and capacities varied from a quarter of a pint (0.14 litres) to a gallon (4.5 litres).

A presentation inkstand dated 1877. The ball might serve as a wafer or stamp box and the bails as a pen rack.

Two pewter capstan-shaped inkwells. These were originally designed like the one on the right for use in ships and later modified like the one on the left for banks and post offices.

INKWELLS AND INKSTANDS

The form of the inkwell was determined by necessity. Its base was solid for the sake of stability. The well was fairly shallow so that only the quill point could be inked and the neck was narrow to prevent evaporation and keep out dust and other impurities.

The earliest inkwells were made of wood, stone or pottery, and some of these date back to the first and second centuries. At the beginning of the seventeenth century pewter inkwells were introduced and the most popular shape, the 'capstan' inkwell, was first designed for use in ships, hence the wide saucer-like base to prevent spillage. This patent design was used right up to the beginning of the twentieth century in banks, post offices and government offices.

The beginning of the nineteenth century saw an increase in literacy and inkwells of a more gracious style were now made in porcelain at the Bow and Chelsea factories, and also by Meissen and Sèvres. Examples of these can be seen in museums, but they rarely appear on the market. The demand grew and by the middle of the nineteenth century there was

a vast array of different types in use. Every possible shape and material were used, from wood to crystal, pewter and gold. Many types had hinged lids, often in brass or silver.

Pressed glass and cut glass inkwells were mass-produced in the second half of the nineteenth century and are probably the best items on which to base a collection. Coloured glass inkwells from the late nineteenth century in blue, green, amber and vaseline are quite rare but worth looking for. Decorated pottery, china, majolica and porcelain inkwells were also made in large quantities and are quite easy to find. Not only English but French, German and Dutch examples can be found, such as French faience ones with their unusual patterns, which vary from region to region, and Delft inkwells, with their distinctive blue and white design. The collector's dream is of finding French inkwells made at the factory of Sèvres. In Germany, Meissen, commonly known as Dresden, made interesting examples, which are much sought after and expensive, and towards the end of the nineteenth century there was a mass

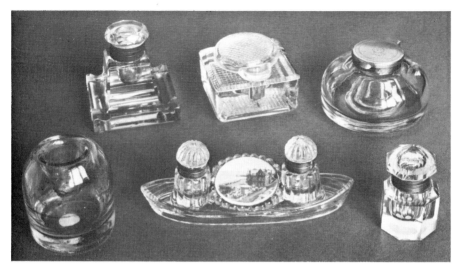

production of export souvenirs in such places as Thuringia, a German equivalent of the Staffordshire potteries. In England, Victorian ladies loved pretty china inkwells, so the factories of Derby and Worcester went to work to produce a wide range of wells, many of which can be found today.

Bronze and brass inkwells were common in the nineteenth century and very many of these metal inkwells have survived and can be found in many shapes and sizes. The Victorians were very inventive and loved gadgets, so the inventors of the day had an eager market and consequently patented many unusual designs such as the Isobath inkwell, the fountain inkwell and the much rarer snail inkwell. Novelty shapes abounded – crouching bears carved in wood, strutting hens cast in spelter (zinc), brass turtles and grinning human faces (the open mouth admitting ink and pen).

Silver was used widely in the manufacture of inkwells, and from the early nineteenth century such craftsmen as Paul De Lamerie, Robert Hennel and Paul Storr made fine examples, but for the present-day collector silver inkwells are very expensive. A better objective would be the silver-topped or silver-mounted inkwells of the nineteenth century. These are fairly plentiful, moderately priced and in an endless variety of shapes.

ABOVE: *Glass inkwells can be found in scores of different shapes. The hinges and tops are usually made of brass, but some can be found in silver. The two-bottle set, one bottle for red ink, the other for black, is a typical seaside holiday souvenir.*

BELOW: *This bell-shaped inkwell has an aperture for the pen on the unseen side. The top screws on, so that the contents are unspillable. The registered number indicates that the design was registered for copyright protection in 1899.*

14

ABOVE: *(from left) A porcelain inkwell with a transfer-printed design, made in Vienna about 1890 and signed Angelica Kauffman; a man's head inkwell of china, made in England about 1860; a pottery inkwell made by Royal Doulton.*

BELOW: *A lady's smiling face and a seated Turk serving as inkwells.*

Travelling inkwells were popular with Victorians so that they could write letters on their travels. Some were made to fit a waistcoat pocket or a lady's handbag. Different shapes and styles were produced: the most common and widely used were neat leather-bound boxes which contained a small glass bottle. The hinged top of the box would contain a spring seal, which when closed formed a watertight carrying container. These can still be found without too much difficulty.

Dual-purpose inkwells also exist. They are often heavy and globular, being made of thick glass, and were intended to serve as paperweights as well as inkwells.

An inkstand, originally called a standish, was a form of cruet for writing utensils. Manufacturers from the seventeenth century supplied an expanding market with attractive matching sets varying in size, composition and materials. In addition to one or two inkwells, the tray of an inkstand would often carry a pounce pot, with a perforated top, holding pounce (powdered pumice) or fine sand to dry the writing, a box for sealing wafers or wax and a taper or candle stand to hold the taper to melt the wax. Sometimes a penknife, a pen-wiper, a small letter rack or a bell to summon a servant might be included.

Every inkstand in silver had its counterpart in Sheffield plate, a sandwich of copper between layers of silver that cost about one third the price of silver and was just as handsome, lacking only hallmarks. French inkstands were often embellished with painted scenes. Viennese ones were made of bronze, sometimes featuring animals or replicas of monuments such as Trajan's Column in Rome. Victorians liked inkstands in gold-plated brass and these often had porcelain inkwells and pounce pots. Brass alone was an excellent metal for making quite elaborate inkstands and Victorian specimens are still quite common. It was often combined not only with porcelain but with wood, marble or glass.

The introduction of the penny post and the growth of literacy made letter writing popular with all classes, and less expensive inkstands were made of polished woods with ebony or black-painted edges, cut glass wells, a brass carrying handle and a drawer for spare pens, stamps, nibs and stationery. Inkstands in Tunbridge ware are very attractive and are fairly easy to find but inkstands in Mauchline ware, which have sycamore lids on inkwells decorated with transfer pictures in black, are much rarer.

As interest in competitive sports increased inkstands were designed for presentation as trophies. These are not usually expensive when the athlete concerned was of only local repute. Those made for national heroes tend to be much more costly.

Two fountain inkwells. The one on the left is a patented 'Bobby' of about 1890, with a green pressed glass base and a clear glass top. The one on the right has a brass base, glass top and a pewter lid.

ABOVE: *A rare French inkwell of three pivoting snails.*

RIGHT: *The snails pivoted outwards for use.*

17

ABOVE: *Inkwells like the two on the left were carried by Victorians for recording travel impressions while journeying. Both fastened securely and would not spill although carried in a pocket or handbag. The glass one is so cut and balanced that the last drop of ink can be used up. The silver cap, hallmarked in Birmingham in 1855, is engraved with the owner's initials.*

LEFT: *A plain silver inkwell, a pipe inkwell with a retractable pen in the stem and two shaped like travelling bags.*

BELOW: *Greyhound inkwells. The holes in the base admit the ink and also hold pens when not in use.*

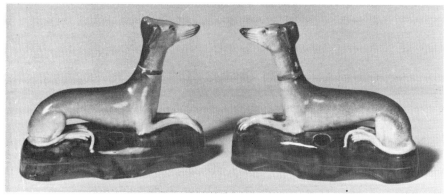

ABOVE: *There are 183 grams (6.5 oz) of weighable silver in this inkstand with two bottles and a candlestick over a wafer box between them. It was made in 1853 by A. J. and N. Creswick and bears a Sheffield assay mark.*

BELOW: *A decorative Tunbridge ware inkstand holding two cut glass wells and a stamp or wafer box with a lift-out lid between them. In front is another lift-out lid over a recess for pens, nibs and so on. The floral pattern on the lids and all four sides is one of the most attractive Tunbridge designs.*

ABOVE: *The hand blotter is in silver and of the type in use today. The tooled leather blotter contained several sheets of blotting paper. Bottom left is a brass hand-shaped paperclip, and to its right is a wooden pounce pot.*

BELOW: *This boxed sealing set has a locking lever on the inkwell so that it can be carried without fear of spilling the ink. The Tunbridge ware barrel is also a sealing set and, like its companion, contains all the items needed for sealing a letter or envelope. Its finial is a taperstick holder.*

Pounce pots. One is in stoneware, of about 1820, and its companion in black basalt is older, about 1790.

POUNCE POTS, PENWIPERS AND SEALS

Vellum, made from calfskin, was one of the earliest materials for writing on and it needed to have surface grease removed before it would take ink. Powdered pumice was found ideal for this, and it proved equally useful for drying ink before the writing blurred on paper which was not treated with size. It was kept in a pounce pot, which was usually drum-shaped, with a top pierced with holes and concave so that the powder could be poured back after use. Some wooden ones had a hole in the lid with a stopper which could be removed for pouring or used to revolve the lid to open a hole in the side. Silver ones are quite rare and in most instances formed part of an inkstand.

Blotting paper, invented accidentally when a workman forgot to add size to the paper mixture, appeared about 1840. Pounce pots were no longer needed and desk blotters appeared, often in folder form in tooled leather or with papier-mâché covers decorated with hand painting or mother of pearl inlay. Hand blotters also had a vogue, either as separate items or as part of a desk set. Particularly popular were those with curved bases, to which the blotting paper was secured, and a knob handle, by which they could be rocked over the paper. Both types became much less common when quick-drying inks and, later, ballpoint pens came on to the market.

Until inks were improved they clogged both quills and nibs, which needed constant wiping or scraping. Small brushes, bristles upwards, either in plain bases or represented as the back bristles of animals, were used, but much more common, though few have survived, were penwipers made from circular pieces of black velvet, neatly bound and sewn together in the middle, with two or three pieces of black cloth between them, made by young Victorian girls as presents for friends and relatives.

Until envelopes were invented letters

ABOVE: *Seals. The small seal (top left) holds a bloodstone engraved with the word 'L'Amitie' and is mounted in gold. Below is an agate with a coat of arms, similarly mounted. The largest seal is of brass and so is the small one, top right, engraved with a rose. The seal on the right is pewter, bearing the intertwined initials E.B.*

LEFT: *A penwiper in brass.*

had to be folded and then sealed down with moistened wafers of flour mixed with gum and non-poisonous colouring matter. These were generally red, but black ones were available for use on mourning stationery. Later sealing wax superseded wafers (which would not take a seal) and inkstands were made including a taperstick and midget candles. The stick of sealing wax was held in the flame of the candle until a blob of wax dropped on to the envelope for the seal's imprint.

Wealthy people might personalise their correspondence by impressing their seals on the wax, thus embossing a motto or sentimental message. Businessmen might have a set of seals mounted wheel fashion, each one bearing a different wording or date. Ladies could buy exquisite boxed sets containing a number of seals made from semi-precious stones which could be screwed on to an accompanying silver or jewelled handle. Boxes equipped with pen, inkwell, sealing wax, taperstick, personal seal and, in a few instances, a musical box that played a short tune were popular presents. Separate tapersticks could be bought.

Many men preferred to wear their seals on a watch chain so that they were immediately ready for use. These were set in gold or silver or, less often, pinchbeck (imitation gold), brass or pewter. The gold was rarely solid metal, a shell being quite adequate for holding the seal, and consequently very few are hallmarked. Cheaper than any of these are the seals on handles, seal and handle being made from one piece of brass.

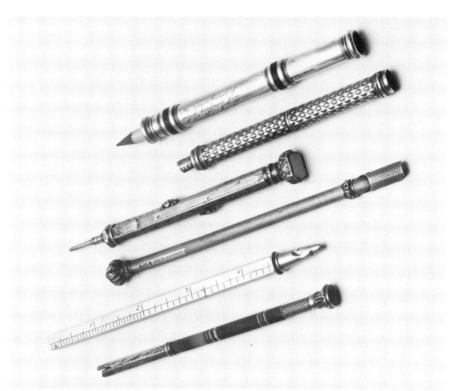

Propelling pencils and pens. The top one, by Sampson Mordan, is in gold and inscribed 'In remembrance of much kindness from Dorothy Nevill'. The two below it are in silver as is the penholder, and that serving as a ruler is in ivory. Below that is a penholder made of agate.

PENCILS

Lead pencils are made of graphite, first discovered in the reign of Elizabeth I, near Keswick, Cumbria, where a new industry started. About twenty different processes are involved in making a pencil, which is 7 inches (178 mm) long and, manufacturers claim, will draw a line 120 miles (193 km) long or write forty-five thousand words before becoming unusable. Most are hexagonal or round and in only the cheapest brands is the cedarwood casing not coloured. So few pencils survive constant sharpening that antique ones are very scarce. Those in short flat silver cases appeal to collectors.

In 1858 Hyman L. Lipman realised that a built-in rubber would save time and might be popular. He made a quick fortune and his rubber tip is a reminder that simple ideas often produce big profits.

The fact that lead pencils needed frequent sharpening and were not intrinsically appealing suggested that there was a market for something that retained its point and looked smart. In 1822 Sampson Mordan invented his Everpointed Pencil, its lead being propelled by pushing a small projection on the casing or by twisting a knob that turned a spiral inside the case. Soon he registered his mark at the Goldsmiths' Hall in order to make pencils in gold and silver. These proved very popular and he went on to produce novelties in the shape

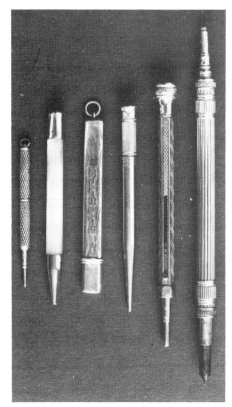

of whisky bottles, axes, swords, Egyptian mummies, spinning tops, likenessess of John Bull, owls, fish, pistols, rifles, whistles, hunting horns and screws. In others he incorporated a perpetual calendar, a clinical thermometer, a money box for small coins and other novelties. At a sale at Sotheby's in Belgravia in 1979 an auctioneer's gavel, a crucifix, a presentation trowel, an owlet, a decanter, an acorn, a locket, a piglet, a tennis racquet, a rowing boat, a table knife and a fish, all made by Mordan, were sold. Production lasted until 1941, when the factory was destroyed by bombing. Although there is a wide enough range of Mordan pencils on which to base a specialist collection, there were countless other manufacturers of propelling pencils of all descriptions, many of them still reasonably priced.

LEFT: *The two pencils with top rings came from chatelaines. Second from the left is a pencil with a mother of pearl barrel with finial and point in 9 carat gold. That on the extreme right is a combined pen and pencil, each being retracted or brought into view by moving the silver bands up or down the ribbed barrel.*

BELOW: *Most stamp cases and boxes were made for home use but this one, with sections for four different denominations, glazed lid and brass fittings, was probably intended for office use.*

The book-shaped box at the top is a Vesta box for holding matches combined with a stamp compartment behind one of its covers. The Tunbridge ware box, of recent date, bears only a simple design and a real Edward VIII stamp. The home-made box on the far right, book-shaped but opening matchbox style, was decorated with needlework and has a 'postage stamp' label on its spine. The miniature envelopes are of silver, the larger having compartments for two different denominations.

WRITING ACCESSORIES

The introduction of the penny post in 1840 added the stamp box to the growing number of writing accessories. The first stamps were imperforate and had to be cut from the sheet. Purchasers usually separated them at once, keeping them in small boxes made for the purpose. Tunbridge ware boxes are the most familiar. This ware, despite its appearance, was not made on the mosaic principle. A coloured pattern was prepared on squared paper and copied in wood by gluing together a large number of thin hardwood sticks of varying colours and shapes so that the same design ran through the solid block thus created. Veneers were then cut from it and glued to the wooden objects to be decorated.

Some of the boxes had a real 'Penny Red' securely varnished on to the lid but the best had the Queen's head in the pattern, made up of hundreds of tiny pieces. From Scotland came tartan ware circular stamp boxes covered completely with a named tartan pattern, their function being revealed by a stamp on the lid.

At first stamp boxes were made to hold only the one value that was available, but as other denominations were issued boxes with several compartments were made. Brass stamp boxes had shallow curved compartments to facilitate taking out stamps. Slim, stamp-sized silver cases, shaped like envelopes, were designed to hold only a few stamps and many had a ring attached for carrying on a watch chain or chatelaine. A few are twice the usual size to accommodate two different values.

Names and addresses might be underlined with a small ruler made in Tunbridge ware, tartan ware, ivory or wood. Tunbridge ware rulers were usually

This cast iron paperweight of a Canadian National Railways locomotive was distributed at the British Empire Exhibition, Wembley. Under the base are details about the size of this giant engine.

6 or 9 inches (152 or 228 mm) long, each inch space having a different pattern. A tartan ware ruler would be slim and bear only the named plaid colours. Some wooden ones, intended for children perhaps, were tubular and had a rubber fitted into one end and a pencil into the other.

Quite rare are cylindrical rulers bearing information about postal charges. They were used in conjunction with a set of postal scales with the appropriate charges engraved on them. Some models included an ivory plaque on the stand on which alterations to postage rates could be printed, saving the purchase of a new set of scales. Quite useful, too, were pocket scales working on the spring balance principle.

Victorian paperclips were the ancestors of the bulldog clip rather than of the small wire office clips used today. The most attractive were made in brass in a variety of sizes and shapes: the most sought-after shape now is probably the hand.

The finest paperweights came from the French factories of Clichy, Baccarat and St Louis and these are rare and expensive, but so many others were made, particularly in glass and base metal, that it is not difficult to start a worthwhile collection. Shallow glass moulds, circular, square, octagonal or obelisk-shaped, were produced showing pictures of holiday resorts and those issued by big firms, especially insurance companies, as reminders to customers, make a very interesting category.

Paperknives for opening letters exist in hundreds of different designs. Large ones

BELOW: *A 6 inch (150 mm) tartan ware ruler. Usually the clan name is printed in gold, slightly enhancing the object's value to collectors, but it is omitted from this piece.*

BOTTOM: *This postal ruler, quite different from typical Mauchline ware, is also a perpetual calendar. On the far side the postal rates of the period are printed.*

ABOVE: *A Victorian letter scale using the Roberval system, made by Halstaff and Hannaford. The scale pans have ceramic inserts painted with female heads, suggesting use by a lady. The weights are missing.*

BELOW: *When envelopes with gummed edges became popular gum pots were no longer needed. This one, mounted in silver, still has its own brush and once formed part of a desk set.*

were for use on uncut newspapers. Blades do not allow for much variation except in the materials used, such as silver, tortoiseshell, mother of pearl, wood and ivory, but the handles were made in fanciful shapes, often with finials in semi-precious stones. Less common are stamp and envelope dampers, consisting of a glass or pottery roller revolving in its well. Pencil sharpeners have not changed much over the years except as amusing shapes for children. More interesting to collectors, perhaps, are those intended for office use.

With penknives variety comes from the casing, which may be in steel, silver, occasionally gold, mother of pearl, tortoiseshell or tartan ware, both plain and patterned. A few incorporate small button hooks for ladies wearing long buttoned gloves.

Desk gum pots, when silver-mounted, are both attractive and useful and should include a small brush. Pen trays in glass, pottery, Mauchline ware, papier-mâché and brass are not hard to find. Less frequently seen are pen boxes with their charmingly decorated lids.

A calendar was essential for correspondence and these exist in many forms. Wooden ones may have rollers that reveal separately the day of the week, date and month. Silver ones usually contain cards for each month so that the appropriate one can be shown at the front. Some freak metal calendars were made to last several years, while ingenious models were 'perpetual'.

In a house with a large family, letters for the post might be dropped into a large wooden letter box standing on the hall table. Some were miniature street pillar boxes, but most were boxlike, perhaps with a domed top, a slot bearing the message 'Letters' and, surprisingly these days, a printed reminder that the 'Post leaves at . . . on Sundays'. These letter boxes were usually sold by large shops and department stores. A mansion or a stately home needed a much larger model, like the 'Victorian-style red lacquered octagonal pillar box with finial and foliate moulded top, 54 inches (1372 mm) high', recently sold at Christie's, South Kensington.

Three Persian pen boxes, the topmost decorated with panels of birds and butterflies among sprays of flowers and two panels showing European ladies. The middle one shows country scenes, while the third has pictures of dervishes in pairs separated by single figures.

A Regency brass-bound writing box with fitted interior, candle stands at the sides and a drawer on one side for an inkwell.

WRITING DESKS

Businessmen tended to use massive desks, some of which accommodated two partners, one at each side. Ladies were more likely to use a *bonheur du jour,* a small, light writing desk with central drawer in front and tiered shelves and cupboards at the back, or the larger Carlton House desk, a writing table with several levels of drawers at back and sides of the work surface. In humbler homes the lady probably owned a davenport, invented by Gillows for a customer of that name. This had a sloping top mounted on a cupboard with drawers at one side and sometimes at the back also.

Throughout the nineteenth century another item which was widely used was the travelling desk (or writing box), which made a leathered or velvet slope when the lid was opened and rested on the table, over compartments for holding stationery. At the higher end was a removable pen tray (spare nibs and holders could be kept under it) with screwtop inkwells, usually of glass, on each side. The more expensive versions sometimes had secret drawers or compartments. The origin is obscure, but it was possibly based on the military dispatch box.

Towards the middle of the nineteenth century wooden writing boxes were being produced to meet an enormous demand. They came in all sizes and were commonly made in mahogany, burr walnut, rosewood and more expensive ones in Coromandel wood. They were made to various specifications. An army officer posted to the North West Frontier would want one robustly built, heavily brass bound, with brass-mounted corners and edges. A Victorian lady, however, might have one made in Tunbridge ware or even papier-mâché. More expensive ones had serpentine lids, sometimes inlaid with

intricate designs in brass or a shield for the owner's initials. Simpler 'tourist writing cases' were sold in Morocco leather, lined with satin, and were equipped with different sizes of stationery, pens, pencils and a paperknife, but not with an inkwell.

Another useful adjunct was the wooden stationery cabinet that in some instances held inkwells as well as writing paper and envelopes, and perhaps an adjustable calendar. The cheapest had no lids but more expensive models had roll-top covers or were made in casket form with elaborate metal hinges, escutcheon plate and corner supports.

TOP: *A French writing slope incorporating a rack for stationery. Its lid, richly decorated with brass inlay, descends in serpentine curves.*

LEFT: *Most pencil sharpeners are small and often gimmicky. Those designed for office use were made so that the pencils were inserted from the side. In this complicated-looking model the pencil goes in at the top.*

ABOVE: *An elaborate Victorian mahogany and floral marquetry stationery box with a fall front. This box includes not only the usual compartments but a set of postal scales and weights.*

BELOW: *This portable writing set was possibly used by a commercial traveller or surveyor. The leather wallet was for stationery and would wrap round the box and, fastened with a ribbon, would stop the contents of the box from spilling.*

FURTHER READING

Rivera, Betty and Ted. *Inkstands and Inkwells.* Crown Publishers Inc, New York, 1973.
Whalley, Joyce Irene. *Writing Implements and Accessories.* David and Charles, 1975.

THE WRITING EQUIPMENT SOCIETY

This society is devoted to the conservation and study of writing instruments and accessories. It publishes a journal, holds meetings and encourages the exchange of information and artefacts among members. Secretary: Miss M. L. Greenland, 4 Greystones Grange Crescent, Sheffield, South Yorkshire S11 7JL, UK.

PLACES TO VISIT

Abbey House Museum, Kirkstall, Leeds, West Yorkshire LS5 3GH. Telephone: Leeds (0532) 755821.

Bath Postal Museum, 8 Broad Street, Bath, Avon BA1 5LJ. Telephone: Bath (0225) 60333.

Birmingham Museum of Science and Industry, Newhall Street, Birmingham B3 1RZ. Telephone: 021-236 1022. (The Charles Turner Collection of writing implements.)

Chepstow Museum, Gwy House, Bridge Street, Chepstow, Gwent NP6 5EZ. Telephone: Chepstow (02912) 5981.

Cumberland Pencil Museum, Southey Works, Keswick, Cumbria CA12 5NG. Telephone: Keswick (0596) 73626.

The Red House Museum, Quay Road, Christchurch, Dorset BH23 1BU. Telephone: Christchurch (0202) 482860.

Shaftesbury Local History Museum, Gold Hill, Shaftesbury, Dorset. Telephone: Shaftesbury (0747) 2157.

ACKNOWLEDGEMENTS

Sincere thanks are due to the following for their help in the preparation of this book: Peter Isbell, who took most of the photographs; Cumberland Graphics, for information; Barbara Colclough, for typing the manuscript; Magna Carta Antiques, Jo Bromhead, Eleanor Johnson, Regency House Antiques, Ivor Robertshaw and Anthony Searle, for loan of material. Photographs are acknowledged as follows: W. and T. Avery Ltd, page 27 (top); Bernson's International Press Service, page 2; Bonham's, Auctioneers, page 23; Christie's South Kensington, Auctioneers, pages 9, 19 (bottom), 29, 31 (top); His Nibs, pages 3, 4 (bottom), 5, 6, 7 (both), 8 (top), 11, 14 (top); Eleanor Johnson, page 24 (bottom); Parker Pen Company Ltd, page 8 (bottom); Phillips, Auctioneers, pages 12, 28, 31 (bottom); Regency House Antiques, Walton-on-the-Hill, Surrey, page 30 (top); Ivor Robertshaw, page 21; Sotheby's Belgravia, Auctioneers, page 19 (top); J. Stone, page 30 (bottom).